Turtle to Butterfly
A Journey through
My Self Discovery

Greta E. Moon

Copyright © 2014 Greta Moon

All rights reserved. This book or any portion thereof may not be reproduced or used in any manner whatsoever without the express written permission of the publisher.

Collaboration:

Editor: Shavonna Bush-All Write Editing

ISBN-13: 978-1941749166
ISBN: 194174916X
**4-P Publishing
Chattanooga, TN
37421**

DEDICATIONS

Terry Hall you helped me see the butterfly within me.

Corri Bischer you love me for who I am and helped me move into position so that I could enter into my cocoon.

Dr. David Banks, Phd. for becoming a spiritual father and teaching me that I have a purpose in the earth.

Laura Brown for being a great leader and helping to draw out the words for this book through S.W.A.T. book writing camp.

Ricky Cintron for telling me every day I am beautiful.

Every reader who is searching for the butterfly within. I'm ready for you to soar.

CONTENTS

1	Turtle	Pg. 9
2	Mouse	Pg. 15
3	Ostrich	Pg. 19
4	Deer	Pg. 23
5	Cat	Pg. 27
6	Lion	Pg. 33
7	Elephant	Pg. 37
8	Horse	Pg. 41
9	Butterfly	Pg. 45

PREFACE

The inspiration for this book came about from a doodle that Corri Bischer had drawn in representation of my transformation. At the time I had not even planned on writing a book about my self-discovery. Somehow, I could not escape the fact that my life had been changing very rapidly over the last year. The initial book plans were scrapped and Corri's doodles took on new life as I began to accept the fact that this book needed to be written if I wanted to go forward in my journey through life. The doodle then became the focus of this process of self-discovery and it mirrored my own personal journey. As the title signifies, Turtle to Butterfly, the process was very slow for me. I didn't begin the process until I was in my early forties. My sincere hope is that you do not have to begin the process so late in life.

As you go through the chapters I want you to understand this book and in your own life journey is not necessarily linear. You may experience parts of this journey more than once or some not all. This book is not necessarily to be understood that your life will proceed as each chapter is aligned, because our journeys are very different. We experience life at different paces and even view them in different ways. I wrote this book about my self-discovery so that you understand that you are not alone in the process. There are people out there that have had experiences similar to your own.

My desire is for you come to a place of freedom to experience life in its fullest. You must surrender yourself to the process of metamorphosis to become the beautiful butterfly waiting to be released. I am excited to see at the end of your journey all your gifts and talents that will be expressed as the sun hits your wings.

Stay in touch and let me know how you have become a beautiful butterfly: turtletobutterfly@gmail.com

I love you all,

Greta E. Moon

Turtle to Butterfly: A Journey Through My Self Discovery

1 TURTLE

"BEHOLD THE TURTLE. HE MAKES PROGRESS ONLY WHEN HE STICKS HIS NECK OUT." JAMES B. CONANT

The turtle stays safely hidden away in his shell from any danger that comes his way. He slowly makes it from one destination to the next at its own pace. Most of my life I have hidden inside a seemingly impenetrable shell of safety. The very first memory of retreating began with my mother asking me not to kiss her anymore. She told me my lips were too wet and not to kiss her again until they were dry, she then wiped the kiss away. I understand now that this is where I began to shape how I felt about who I was as a person. This alone may have not been damaging enough within itself, but many instances of my mother's disapproval would continue. I could never measure up to her mountainous standards. In my eyes, my mother was like God. She held the power of my life and death in her hands. In her words and actions I lived in this shadow of fear until I left home at seventeen.

I believed my adoptive mother was supposed to give me a life filled with love. Instead, I was offered a life of fear and rejection. I believe what saved me from insanity was a rebellious streak. I remember from the time I was able to read I would go to the library and read about child rearing. In the midst of one of her furious storms, I would tell her about what the experts would say about raising children. I was going to make sure she knew she was wrong in the way she would discipline me and my brothers. Subconsciously, I would cause my mother's anger to be transferred to me so that in a sense my brothers would be protected. I became the Harriet Tubman in my family. I learned how to run away and where to run to. I then taught my brothers how to run away to safety. Perhaps that wasn't the best way to handle the situation, but it taught my brothers how to fight back.

Turtle to Butterfly: A Journey Through My Self Discovery

When I left home at seventeen I vowed never to be hurt again and to never hurt my children the same way my mother hurt me. This vow began the full manifestation of retreating fully into my shell. Although I went on to marry and have children I still lived in my own very private world. I threw myself into work and when I wasn't working I would spend hours studying the Bible. This seemed to me the perfect set up for life. I had my family and then was able to retreat into my shell when I was ready. I never abused my children physically, but I believe I neglected them emotionally because I never let them get emotionally close. I believed they suffered in that sense. Until this day I see the disconnectedness in our interactions with each other.

After I separated from my husband I got into a relationship that could have had the potential of being damaging. The guy was very sweet, but an ex-drug addict. He had his own demons he was running from and I spent more time, I feel, trying to support him than on healing myself. During that relationship I got pregnant. I was disillusioned with the thought perhaps this was going make our relationship better. That thinking process didn't last long because I miscarried the baby at 12 weeks into my pregnancy and shortly thereafter I walked away from him. In midst of being depressed about losing my baby, River Zane, the troubles with my ex-husband were quickly becoming a firestorm. He moved to another state and the children visited him for the holidays. One Christmas they were visiting him. He called to tell me he was not going to let them come home. Although my girls eventually came home he convinced my son to stay with him. I not only loss my unborn child, but my youngest son.

I was once again at the brink of suicide and trying to figure out if I started drinking again how I could I hide it. In that haze of rage, depression, defeat, and confusion I decided that I was going to move to where my ex-husband was to at least be close to my son. This move would prove critical in my metamorphosis even though I would not see its manifestation for seven years.

After the move I stayed angry, but the depression began to dissipate, and the confusion began to clear. I started picking up the pieces and found a job that I could stay within my shell, but still be in control. There was a guy that I worked with that was quiet and kept to himself. He asked me to go out and our relationship grew. It was a relationship in which I was very comfortable because no demands were put on me to function outside of my shell. God began whispering sweetly into my spirit about a year and a half into our relationship beckoning me slowly from my shell. The changes began to show in my life and in the relationship. I took a vow of purity which would change the dynamics of the relationship and how I viewed myself. The death of the relationship came when I decided that I wanted to be alone until God healed my heart. My boyfriend became frustrated because he could not understand why this change was important. Honestly, I didn't understand at the time either, but I knew my heart could not belong to both. God was not only testing my heart, but my readiness to move forward. It was essential for me to embrace the move to be released from this prison of a shell. The greatest obstacle to my transformation was realizing that everyone was not out to hurt me. Every relationship including this one after my divorce reinforced in my mind, that relationships will always be hurtful. This behavior extended into avoiding developing friendships as well.

Now that I had chosen to walk away from unhealthy relationships I could hear God's voice much clearer. Still one question remained, "How could God heal such brokenness? He would very quickly answer this by beginning the healing on my calloused heart with the balm of His sweet love.

The shell I created retarded my ability to interact with others emotionally, I lacked in social skills, and my spiritual growth was stunted. Year after year I continued to hide within this shell not knowing that I was crippling myself to the death if I didn't have a God epiphany. This came at the age of 42 when I began to understand my life was empty and I was alone. The first indication that something was changing in life was the expansion of my influence at work through rapid promotions to higher positions. Still my motto was to do whatever I could to stay in my shell. I was happy staying under the radar, but I believed He moved me into a position that I had to physically see my influence. Opportunities arose to speak in trainings, join organizations, and build friendships. I understood that I had to submit to the process of His drawing me outward to move forward.

He began to bring people into my life that sincerely cared about me and a church that teaches about having purpose. It wasn't just a passive message it was an expectation to walk in your purpose. This circle of friends and church teaching were what would catapult me into transformation.

Are you hidden within the prison of your own shell? Are you afraid to come out of this because of circumstances that have occurred in your life? It may seem impossible to change from your vantage point. Come out of hiding. Change is right before you if you just stick your neck out. You must come to a point where you become tired of being isolated. There is a choice to be made to become fearless. I had to tell myself, "I am unique and needed in the earth not to just exist, but to live. There is so much more to life and living fully." You are cheating yourself just as I cheated myself from becoming the person you are designed for in the earth. You must not believe anything less. There is a great contribution in the earth that you have to offer. There are many people that need to hear your story just as you are hearing mine.

Moving forward and sticking your neck out will not be easy. Hurt may come, but the thing to remember is not to retreat. Every day you need to assert yourself telling yourself that all will be well. This is the first step to beginning a new chapter in your life. However, you must be willing to allow change to come. Every day is new chance to see life with new lenses. In every aspect of my life I made conscious decisions to do everything different. Especially since I waited so long to change it would have been easy to slip back into that shell of safety. I pray that this book reaches you sooner than later, so the struggle will not be so great. You may even want to delay changing because of fear. My strong advice is face the fear head on. How can you get started? The greatest thing you have is the power of deciding to change. During this process, be brutally honest because if you are not, you will set yourself up to being stuck in this shell only to die there. This will be the greatest adventure you take, but you have to be bold and fearless.

1. What do I fear most in my life right now? Why?

2. What are you doing to change the things you fear?

3. What do you have to lose if you come out of your shell?

"For the Holy Spirit, God's gift, does not want you to be afraid of people, but to be wise and strong, and to love them and enjoy being with them."
                1 Timothy 1:7-The Living Bible

Turtle to Butterfly: A Journey Through My Self Discovery

2 MOUSE

"QUICK IS THE MOUSE TO RUN WHEN FEAR ABOUNDS."
GRETA MOON

The typical mouse is nocturnal; staying in the burrow until nightfall. Once night has fallen he ventures out to find food. If he senses danger near he runs back into the burrow until he is certain that the it has passed. Once the process of coming out of hiding began for me there were many days I would rather stay safely in the burrow because the fear seemed suffocating and even crippling. It seemed best to stay in the burrow never to venture out again.

The years of my life spent in that shell had caused a type of social and relationship atrophy. I could not develop any type of lasting relationships because fear impeded the entire process. In my mind, I created the scenario my peers saw me as strange and different to excuse myself from relationships. I must admit at times interacting in conversations were strained. I would stumble over my words, break into the conversations in odd points, and sometimes just stand there as an observer. I often wondered, "How was I ever going to be "normal?"

I had to come to a resolution that those things that were hindering me were what I needed to use as a platform for growth. One helpful tool was to place myself into situations in which I had no other choice, but to interact with others. This became a confidence booster because it helped me to conquer the fear that tried to overtake me.

One time that I used this tool was at a meeting at our church. During the meeting we brought information on how we are impacting our area of expertise. Initially, I would come to these forums and present some general information, when it required you to relay something with more depth information. Prior to the next meeting I vowed to be ready and unafraid. I typed up the opportunities that I had been involved in and what was coming. The round table began and my turn to speak came way too fast. I pulled my list out and began to speak. It was not the speech of a great orator, but I was able to deliver the message. No one could tell that I wanted to run into the burrow to hide.

During this part of the journey sometimes fear will try to overtake you as flood. You may even feel like your drowning. Many times I felt like I was gasping for air beneath the waves of fear. Force yourself to rise to the top of these waves by seeing the reality of the situation. You must see that all fear is not life threatening and oftentimes there is nothing to fear.

Another crucial element during this part of the journey is to begin developing solid healthy relationships. This will be necessary to understand that you are valuable as a person. I owe a great deal to a woman that came to work for me at the daycare that I work as a director. She became a very dear friend who saw into my heart. It was almost as if she knew the remedy to draw me from deep within the burrow of fear. One of the first things she did was to invite me to try out for a local women's contact football league. This was a compounded situation because not only had I in my adulthood never had a friend; I never played sports either. Well, I threw myself head long into both. The friendship was beneficial because I knew she valued me and all my quirkiness. She taught me how to see myself through the lenses of others. Joining the football team caused me to learn how to value my unique abilities. It also taught me that I did not have to "fit" into a certain mold. Everyone on the team had their strengths and weaknesses. They all brought something different to making the team a whole.

You and I both have unique gifts and talents that are as precious as gold. If we continue to run we are not only cheating ourselves, but those who will benefit from our unique gifts and talents. You may have attempted to come out of the burrow previously, but ran back in feeling defeated. The opportunity is still there waiting. The only thing that must change is the environment in which freedom is found. You may ask, "How I can change the environment?" The environment changes through the lens in which you look through. The environment of fear is conquered through asserting yourself in confidence. We often begin to possess fear as a lifestyle. Everything we say and do becomes based on the fear that we believe will manifest. Bring on the friendships, opportunities to join groups, and advance forward at work or ministry. Conquer the fear by no longer accepting that running like the mouse is acceptable. This process is ongoing even after you believe that you have been freed to soar as the butterfly. You will begin to experience many new opportunities after you decide to stop running.

Retreating into our safe places will be the easiest at this point in the journey because it has been our best friend, comforter, and source of life. I caution you that retreating will be detrimental to your success on this journey. Take a stand against the fear and stand firm. I mentioned this process will be trying because you are going to be involved in going after a new way of living life, but it will be one of the most rewarding. You will finally get to experience life and freedom. The shadow and darkness of the mouse burrow can no longer hide your beauty. Come forth to experience life the way you were created for in the earth. You were created so beautiful and were never meant to be hidden away. Take control of your life by taking back the feelings of fear and turn them into a victory.

1. List your fears on one side of a sheet of paper and on the other half write why you're afraid. Is it a past or present situation? Honestly, are you allowing these things to remain in your life?

2. What is stopping you from coming out of that place of fear?

3. What are some things that you can do to start the process of coming out of the mouse burrow? This does not have to be some grand step. It can be something as simple as beginning a journal of truths about yourself.

"Yes, be bold and strong! Banish fear and doubt! For remember, the Lord your God is with you wherever you go."
Joshua 1:9-The Living Bible

3 OSTRICH

"AS THE OSTRICH WHEN PURSUED HIDES ITS HEAD, BUT FORGETS HIS BODY; SO THE FEARS OF COWARD EXPOSE HIM TO DANGER."
AKHENATON

The ostrich is known to be the fastest runner over a given period of time. Often time we see the pictures of ostriches with their heads stuck in the sand in representation of procrastination or fear. I would I would run as fast as I could instead of dealing with situations in life and stuck my head in the stand for fear of living life. The enemy saw these as opportunities to stop me from finding out my true potential. He saw me running in the direction of walking in my purpose. He saw the light of understanding my purpose shining ever so brightly upon me. He would cloud out my view with his greatest weapon of fear. He tried to keep me running in fear just like an ostrich so that I wouldn't have time to find out who I was created to be and my purpose in the earth. He has done the same in your life.

The illusion is that with my head in the sand I would have been safe. In reality, I was not safe because the rest of me was exposed. The enemy was standing there at my backside tapping me on my shoulder to remind me of my past failures, fears, and even lies to keep me from moving forward. I had to pull my head out of the sand and stop putting my running shoes on when it appeared that fear wanted to overtake me. I believed if I kept my head in the sand long enough, the things that I feared would disappear and if I ran far enough life would straighten itself out. I hoped that one day the people that hurt me would at least acknowledge the bruises they left on my heart. However, I never confronted them and they, in turn, never acknowledged that they hurt me. In fact, I allowed the people that hurt me to stay in my life. I stayed living in fear and life situations just got worse because I never separated myself from those that wronged me. I continued to nurse the hurts as they came never resolving to cut ties with those relationships.

Fear became crippling because I allowed it to control the boundaries in which I lived. How did I overcome this fear? I took my head out of the sand and confronted it head on. I literally decided to go to another height in life. I went rock climbing. I am not talking about a six-foot-tall wall in an air-conditioned room with safety mattresses on the floor. This rock wall was about forty feet in height. Honestly, I wanted to quit before I ever began. Fear began to take over, my mouth became dry, weakness overwhelmed my body, and tears streamed down my face. Then I climbed one step and then the next, and the next. I looked down at the belayers and they encouraged me every step of the way. After what seemed to be a hundred feet I made it to the top. An overwhelming whoop bellowed out from my exhausted lungs. I sat there breathing not only a sigh of relief, but of victory.

I could have easily quit before I put on the equipment, but it was time to stop hiding from my fear. This is what we must do with situations that we are afraid of in life. They must be confronted. Whatever you are afraid of set out to conquer it. There will be symptoms of fear that show up: struggling with letting go, tears, weakness at heart, and the need to run. Stop. Those are only temporary until the victory comes. You create the victory when you tackle and defeat the fear. Have you ever said to yourself, "If I don't acknowledge the fears they will go away?" This is one of the cruelest lies we tell ourselves. Fear never just goes away. It remains waiting for the opportunity to create more havoc in our lives. It is a lie that we make our own dark reality, but we were never created to live in fear. We must confront fear with boldness to destroy the stranglehold it has on our lives.

Another thing that is necessary is someone to support you in your confrontation of this fear. This is crucial because sometimes the enemy can scream so loud and seemingly blot out the light of victory. It is only a lie that the light is not there and the screams are only as loud as you allow them to be. Life situations don't just straighten themselves out if we hide from what we fear. One of two things are going to happen, your situation is going to stay the same or get worse. We either do nothing to help the situation or we do everything to make it worse. It is almost as if we need to prove to ourselves we have a reason to stay hidden.

I hid from life after the separation and divorce from my ex-husband because the pain seemed too great to bear. The problems that existed in my marriage did not straighten themselves out when I divorced. In fact, they became what seemed to be an unconquerable monster. I got involved with the wrong type of people, walked away from God, and did a lot of things contrary to what I knew was right. Hiding away from life became the most comforting place, but also the most saddening and depressing. Escaping from that darkness seemed formidable. I had to re-evaluate my life and ask some very specific questions like, "Why did I get involved in relationships and situations that were not healthy?" Also, I had to admit that my decisions not only affected me, but also my children because they endured abuse. There will be questions you will have to ask of yourself. To grow you must be brutally honest when you answer. You cannot continually hide in fear from the truth.

The last thing in this part of the process is to stop nursing the wounds. I continually wanted to rehearse my pain over and over. This instilled the idea within myself that I was the victim. This was not true, but it allowed me to live as victim by either being involved in things that caused me to get hurt or by sabotaging relationships. The cycle would have continued if I did not recognize this self-destructive behavior. I had to understand that I am not a victim and you can do the same. We have been designed to be victorious. We must not give away the power instilled within us. Stand firm in the darkness of life say enough is enough and move forward.

This journey of life can be very difficult I am not denying that fact. There is a greater truth that remains. You have a solid rock to stand upon, a promise to succeed, and future full of life and freedom. You were born with everything within you to live in the light. I am calling you to come forth to live above and beyond where you are at presently in life at this point.

1. Which issues are keeping you from taking your head out of the stand? Be brutally honest.

2. How will you deal with each issue? Be specific.

3. What are you holding onto that you must let go? Put a time frame on when you are going to let go. This gives yourself a measurable goal.

"Lord, have mercy on me; all day long the enemy troops press in. So many are proud to fight against me; how they long to conquer me. But when I am afraid, I will put my confidence in you. Yes, I will trust the promises of God. And since I am trusting him, what can mere man do to me."

Psalm 56:1-4-The Living Bible

4 DEER

"THE DEER STANDS EVER SO VIGILANTLY; FRAGILE IN ITS WATCHFULNESS." GRETA MOON

Just as the deer stands at the edge of the field taking caution to the signs of danger. I stood cautiously as I began to enter the field of life. I was still on high alert, vigilantly watching for danger lurking in the hidden places all around. I was eager to break free from the darkness I had been encapsulated by, but to frighten to move forward. There were times I would drop my guard and go to the brook of life and drink deeply quenching the need to be free from isolation. As soon as the leaves rustled with life's soon coming threats I darted back into my world of safety. I longed for a freedom to enjoy life continuously, but at times I could not get beyond living in fear that something or someone may hurt me once again. I remained in that state of fragility because I could be so caught up in watching that I forgot that I must move forward.

This vigilance bred a comfort that I began to accept as the norm. What I thought was a good life became lonely and isolated. I began to believe there was no need to move forward because life was good. I never felt the need to build long lasting relationships because I lived in constant fear of getting hurt. The relationships that I did build were what I called "surface relationships." I could engage in idle chit chat while at work or school then I returned to the safety of my home. I didn't participate fully in those relationships and sometimes I would not share what I felt about a situation because I was afraid my feelings would not be valued. I lived like this for many years because I believed the closer I was to someone the greater the possibility of hurt. The reality is that we may get hurt, but we don't have to become its victim.

Building relationships are essential for us to grow as individuals and to impact the world.

In this stage of the journey be open to take chances on building relationships. You must open up so that other people can get to know who you are. This process can be frightening because of the possibility of rejection, but you need to develop the attitude that if rejection comes it is not because of who you are as a person. Every relationship may not be time worthy or perfect, but I know I gained critical skills in learning how to build relationships. There have been people that have come into my life for a moment and I have learned a great deal about myself and how relationships should or should not work. These relationships are necessary to begin to break down our defenses, so we can move to the next level of personal growth. Once our hearts are softened we are ready to begin to make some lifelong relationships.

You have gifts and talents to offer in relationships that are valuable to other people. Open your heart to the fullness that comes from experiencing solid healthy relationships.

1. Are the threats failure in relationships real or a product of past disappointments?

2. If the threats are real what should you do to be free from them?

3. If they are not real threats, but just a by-product of past disappointments, identify them and explain why you continue to lean on them instead of letting go and moving forward.

4. What are some ways you can begin to build relationships?

5. What will you do if these relationships fail/work?

"Cast your cares on the Lord and He will sustain you; He will never let the righteous be shaken."
> Psalm 55:22-The Living Bible

5 CAT

"THE CAT LIVES ALONE. HE HAS NO NEED OF SOCIETY. HE OBEYS ONLY WHEN HE WISHES, HE PRETENDS TO SLEEP THE BETTER TO SEE, AND SCRATCHES EVERYTHING HE CAN SCRATCH."
CHATEAUBRIAND

The cat is independent, but is in need of acknowledgment. She seeks out attention from the owner only when she is ready. Spending days alone stretching out so comfortably for hours on end during the day is a cat's heaven. Once the owner comes through the door she is at their feet meowing and rubbing her body on their legs. At times the cat will be in full on play mode doing everything to get their attention. On the opposite end of the spectrum the cat will become aggravated if she has not accepted the invitation to be acknowledged. She may lash out in anger scratching and growling letting the owner know that they have gone too far in their advances.

This cat like behavior developed very early in my childhood. I remember at a very young age spending a lot of time alone. I was very independent of people, yet I still wanted validation. I pretended not to care if you were there or not by creating a safe world in which you only entered by special invitation. I paid a high price for creating this world because I became comfortable being alone. Even as an adult I found it difficult to invite others into my life on an emotional and physical level. If you crossed me I would strike out by cutting you out of my life.

The day of my adoption would be the last time that I can remember feeling beautiful or validated by my mother. I can still hear her voice as she spoke saying, "I am going to call you Greta because you are as beautiful as Greta Garbo." It would be just a few years later that my mother began to abuse me and my brother physically, emotionally, and mentally. I never would be able to develop an emotional connection to her even into adulthood. My mother became this fiercely intimidating figure in my life. It is that same intimidation that caused me to fear bonding with other women throughout my life. The physical abuse that we endured was at times brutal. Whatever electrical cord she could lay her hands on became the instrument of torture. I can remember the searing heat of the cord as it made contact with my skin. I would lay there still and quiet counting the number of times the cord made contact. Laying still and quiet would seem impossible, but the stiller and the quieter we were ended the strikes quicker. We were even told we were not allowed to cry. I believe the verbal and emotional abuse left far deeper scars than the physical abuse. I will never forget her "favorite" word to call me was bitch. I did not understand what that meant, but I understood that it was a bad word. For her to call me that meant that I was no better than that. I concluded that I would never do or say enough to make her happy. Even if I couldn't make her happy I hoped at least she could follow through with her promise to love me. I eventually accepted that I would never hear those words, "I love you."

In this world without love I was left starving for attention. In desperation to know that I was loved and accepted I clung to anyone that showed me any type of acceptance. The earliest memory I can recall of feeling as if I was accepted happened during a family vacation. My cousin invited me to stay with her a few days. I finally was good enough for someone to be happy I was around. The first day was happy and carefree as a seven or eight year old could be. Her parents were away at work all day and we had the run of the house. Her big brother was our babysitter and all it seemed that he was asking was that we cleaned up any mess we made. That was no problem for me because my mother was very strict about cleaning when we were at home. As night came the brother made comments about how pretty I was and how smart I was. I had not heard those words in years. My cousin did not give any hint to what would happen over the next few days. This would be the first time I was molested.

I really did not understand what was happening and my cousin would just tell me to do what he said to do. At that moment I was afraid, but I was more afraid of disobeying him. He said he was going to tell my mother I wasn't listening and I was being bad. Of course, I did not want to make my mother upset on vacation because of my disobedience. Also, I really wanted someone to pay attention to me I didn't understand that this kind of attention he was giving was not an appropriate way to show a little girl. Over the three or four days that I stayed every time the parents were not in the house I was subjected to his abuse.

The next time I was molested was just a few short years later. I spent a lot of time at homes of the children that lived in my neighborhood as a place of escape. There was one family that moved in the neighborhood. They had girls that were a few years younger than me. Their parents offered an opportunity to babysit. This was a way to escape my reality to enjoy a home that seemed to be perfect. I babysat on a few occasions and then sometimes I would just go over their house to hang out. The father would still be at home at times and he would give me a hug, pat me on the back, and even kiss me. It seemed at the time very innocent. Just an appreciative dad for a good babysitter. This behavior went on for several weeks, eventually becoming more frequent. At the time I did not understand that he was grooming me for the next stage of molestation. It became a full blown sexual relationship. Although I felt it was wrong I needed to feel I was accepted. I even began to believe the lies that he told me that he loved me and we were going to be together one day.

My mother never knew that I had been molested. At some point I would have been able to tell her, but before that time came we had the "sex talk". I remember that conversation because that was the day that I became ashamed of being molested. My mother in essence said, "that if you had sex you were a whore." I am sure those words have even shaped how I viewed sex as an adult.

These instances would not be last time that I experienced sexual abuse, but I promised after the last time that I was raped at the age of seventeen I would never see myself as a victim. I refused to be hurt so I shut myself off emotionally from other people. I became this stony-hearted woman that lacked almost no outer emotion. The pains of life I learned to stuff so far within they became non-existent and the pains of others became irrelevant. I thought I was protecting myself from being hurt, but my heart became so hard that I couldn't establish relationships. I lost sight of the fact that I still needed people in my life. If you ever experienced this type of deep pain you know we often tend to shut people out, but it is necessary to release the hurt. This allows for the stone upon our hearts to begin to dissolve.

Once that process begins you will no longer find the deep need to be validated by accepting relationships that are not healthy emotionally or physically. The need to justify these relationships to have the illusion of validation by someone else whether it be positive or negative will no longer exist. Remember that you still must look for the red flags that let you know if this is a relationship/friendship that you do not want to keep. You do not have to try and make every relationship work because it may not be good for you. Please, be encouraged that if you are at this place in your life it is not the end. You were created with such beauty and grace. Your past experiences do not dictate who you are as person. They do not dictate the type of future you should experience. Allow those that bring goodness and joy into your life to begin to speak life into those dark places. Trust your instincts. Seek wise counsel if you do not understand some emotions that you may begin to experience.

1. What circumstances have caused you to feel as if you need to be validated by others?

2. What are some behaviors that are keeping you from seeing your true worth?

3. Can you forgive those that hurt you and forgive yourself to allow the past to begin to heal?

4. What are some ways you can you begin to reach out to other people?

5. Write down the things that make you unique? I would suggest even that you look in the mirror each day to rehearse these qualities.

"The Lord is close to those whose hearts are breaking."
Psalm 34:18-The Living Bible

Turtle to Butterfly: A Journey Through My Self Discovery

Turtle to Butterfly: A Journey Through My Self Discovery

6 LION

"AN INJURED LION STILL WANTS TO ROAR."
RANDY PAUSCH

The lion walks across the savanna grasslands leading the pride with fierceness. From birth the lion is set to either remain with the pride or go out independently. The lion that remains must fight the other remaining males at times for his position as the leader. Calculating coldness and decisiveness compels him to retain his position as domineering force of the pride. His independent nature allows for him to push away to roam alone for a lifetime or find a new pride.

During this part of my journey I had already learned to push my family away emotionally at a very young age. This emotionally solitary life helped me learn to become a leader of my own pride, which were my brothers. It was my responsibility to protect them with fierceness. I spent a lot of time at nine and ten years old reading child development books and trying to understand what I believed would be the "proper" way to raise children. I then spewed that information at my adoptive mother just to make her angry enough to turn her attention away from my brothers. I learned to dominate these very intense situations. I made sure that my adoptive mother knew of her failings by disciplining us in such a harsh manner. We fought for the dominating position in our family just as male lions fight. This fight continued until I left home at seventeen wounded and emotionally indifferent.

Being an emotionally solitary child to becoming an adult that lacked outward emotion was not a far jump. My adoptive mother was emotionally indifferent towards us and made it very apparent our feelings were not valued from a young age. I can remember one instance when I was about eleven or twelve my mother asked me to tie my brother up so she could whip him with an extension cord. It was if what I felt about tying him up did not matter. Her only concern was whether the rope came loose. Of course, I was not going to allow my mother to whip him like that. I tied the ropes loose enough that if he wiggled enough he could free himself. This stopped the whipping several times and each time she told me to tie him up again. At one point she left the room to take a break and I told my brother to jump out the window and runaway. I gave him his clothes and told him to come back later for more. The look on my mother's face when she returned back to the family room, in my opinion, was priceless. She asked where he was I responded very calmly that he must have jumped out of the window. I became both of my brothers' mother, protector, and advocate and I had not even came into the fullness of being a teenager.

My fight to be the dominating force I believe was the breeding ground for my mother's hatred toward me. I made a decision that I didn't care if she hated me or not. I was not ever going down without a fight. My mother could say or do what she wanted to me, but I refused to let her ruin their lives. A few months before my seventeenth birthday she repeatedly said the day I turned 17 she was putting me out. She made sure she included how much she could no longer stand to look at my face. Battle weary, I was ready to leave. The last act of infamy would soon come. My brother and I were arguing over a television program that he wanted to watch. He proceeded to unplug his television to carry it upstairs to his room. My mother met him at the top of the stairs as I travelled right behind him in chase. She attempted to shove him down the stairs. I am glad I was right behind him because this could have easily resulted in a serious injury or even death. I pushed him forward and he dropped the television. At the moment, I told my mother how much I hated her and everything she had done to us. She then asked us to get out of her house. I never looked back.

According to state regulations I was not considered an adult at seventeen and my brother was two years younger than myself, so we had to be placed in foster care. This was my first attempt at trying to live a somewhat normal life, but wound up not being the best placement. My foster father attempted to kiss me and touch me inappropriately and at my new high school I felt like an outsider. Once again, I was like the lion roaming outside of a pride. I stayed cold-hearted, I did not make friendships, and kept to myself. Several abusive relationships later and marriage still did not dissolve my stony heart. Being strong willed like the lion I determined that I would lead not needing anyone. In the work place and my own personal life, I was very decisive and domineering just like the lion. I knew what I wanted in life and was going to get to that goal. My lack of emotional connection became a great hindrance. I had moved so many steps forward, but was not approachable. I did not build many relationships because most people did not know what to think of such a cold-hearted person.

I came to a point where I had to understand and accept that I would have to roam in this pride alone if I continued to be so cold hearted. I began to release some of the pain little by little allowing myself to connect with others to build relationships. Just as I have been victorious you can experience this same victory over your past. Your past does not define who you are as person. You have value and have something to contribute in this earth. You carry within your unique gifts and talents to share with others. Your roar that many thought could be silenced still resounds clearly. You are king and victor over all the pain you have experienced.

1. What areas of your life have you dominated to the point that it has caused a lack of growth?

2. Being battle weary what pieces of armor could you begin to take off?

3. Are there emotions that are buried so deep that need to be released?

4. In what ways can you begin to roar again and regain your position as King?

"You have armed me for strong armor for the battle. My enemies quail before me and fall defeated."
Psalms 18:39-The Living Bible

Turtle to Butterfly: A Journey Through My Self Discovery

7 ELEPHANT

"ALL TOO SOON WE FORGET THE THINGS WE THOUGHT WE COULD NOT FORGET. ELEPHANTS BUILD MEMORIES AND HOLDS ONTO THEM."
AUTHOR UNKNOWN

The elephant is such a large creature roaming through the jungle, but so gentle in manner. They move through the forest paths without disturbing anything that lay outside of the paths that they have walked each day. They live in tight knit family communities called herds. They experience several emotions such as joy, anger, and grief. They are very intelligent and have memories that span many years. Their capacity to hold onto memories allows the matriarch to guide the herd to watering holes many miles away. As the elephant, I had not forgotten the painful memories of the past. Many times I thought I would be swallowed by the sheer number of them. It seemed like I lived in a jungle of pain. I could not maneuver through them with ease just as an elephant not disturbing the path of life I had created. Instead of remembering and rehearsing the pain I needed to purge these memories so that I would stop returning to the same type of familiar abusive relationships.

This familiarity of the physical and verbal abuse I experienced as a child was so hard to break free from because I was so beaten down I did not know my own worth. I found myself as an adult being trapped in these same types of relationships. At eighteen I experienced my first emotionally, verbally, and physically abusive relationship. Every day I was told I was nothing and no one cared. He made sure I was isolated from my family and he watched my every move. The defenses that I thought I built up when I left home were quickly shredded. They were no match to fend off memories of the abuse I experienced growing up coupled with the abuse I was experiencing in this relationship. I could no longer fight because I was so tired. This is also when I became addicted to alcohol. In the beginning I drank occasionally when he drank. As the abuse intensified I began to drink more than he did. I could easily consume about six to eight 40 ounce beers in a day. The alcohol did not numb the pain it just gave me something else to think about. I became swallowed up with despair believing that I would never escape this relationship alive. Since I did not see a way I could leave I planned my own escape by suicide. One night after he beat me up and fell asleep in a drunken stupor I had enough of living. In desperation, I went to the front of our apartment and stuck his .22 caliber gun in my mouth. I could not get the trigger to stop sticking. Then I heard my daughter crying in her room. I slumped down defeated once again, but I was grateful because I was there one more day for my daughter. The abuse worsened to the point I ended up in the emergency room unrecognizable and with a severe concussion. The relationship did not end there. He threw me and my daughter out onto the streets one night. I walked the streets with her in my arms until I found a quiet stairwell for us to sleep. The next day I walked about five miles to the homeless shelter for women and children. It took one last attempted and failed suicide and a stay in a hospital mental health ward before I left him. It seemed I could not escape walking on these same paths of familiarity.

I ended up marrying a man that was emotionally abuse towards me. He was also emotionally and physically abuse towards our children. He would bully all of us by throwing tantrums until he got what he wanted. Most of the physical abuse occurred when I left home. When I came home I had to always pick up the pieces of our children's hearts. I chose not to leave him because when I married him I vowed when I would not divorce because that seemed to be the right thing to do. I believe that if I stuck it out and things would get better. I just learned to live with the abuse and taught my children the same thing. After 16 years of marriage I finally had enough of picking up the pieces and I took my children and we left with nothing but the clothes on our backs.

It was only until I could see that this path that I was on was no longer the right choice. I was able to see that the watering hole I continually visited over the years was no longer viable. I had to have enough of him bullying me and the children, not paying bills, our utilities being shut off, landlords knocking on our doors, and going to court for preventable things. Leaving was very frightening because I had no family for support and no place to call home. One strength that I possessed was knowing that I could make it on my own. This kept me encouraged every day. Every step that I moved forward a new life began to form as new paths were travelled.

It is a continual process not to rely on old memories to dictate your life's path. Your past does not dictate what memories you will make in the future. Unlike the elephant, you can move forward from the pain of the past. You can learn your purpose and identity in the earth. New paths await for you to forge ahead to create a happy, healthy, and a joyous life.

1. What pain have you rehearsed that has caused you to stay in unhealthy relationships?

2. What familiar people, places, and things do you find yourself revisiting? Are they helping you to grow as an individual?

3. Are you ready to release the memories of the past?

4. Visualize yourself leaving the old paths behind? Now write down what new paths you will begin to take.

"[Love] keeps no record of wrongs."
2 Corinthians 13:5-New International Version

Turtle to Butterfly: A Journey Through My Self Discovery

8 HORSE

"A MAN ON A HORSE IS SPIRITUALLY AS WELL AS PHYSICALLY BIGGER THAN A MAN ON FOOT."
JOHN STEINBECK

The horse is one of the most intelligent creatures that interact with humans on an emotional level. They are full of beauty, grace, and strength as they move upon the earth. Their spirit and pride show forth when we interact with them. The horse handler must always remember even if a horse is calm and at peace it can easily be provoked to becoming nervous.

I walked through life way beneath how I was created. The lies that kept me in poor relationships, ignorant of my purpose, and stagnant in spiritual growth became my prison. The bit of the enemy controlled my thoughts about myself and life decisions.

The handling of a horse can make or break its spirit. This applies to how we speak over our lives and the lives of others. It is very true our words have power. Sometimes the damage that words create are irreparable. The enemy waits for us to speak words that line up with his agenda to attempt to destroy our lives. Once they are spoken he begins to plant seeds that are cultivated by life's disappointments. Our spirits are broken once the seeds take root and we begin to believe they hold truth in our lives. We all must take care what we speak over others. This is especially important for parents to take care not to speak curses over their children. As I mentioned earlier in the book about the word bitch being my mother's favorite word to call she was not aware of the damage that it would cause. Of all the cruel words that mother spoke to me one still rings loudly in my memory. It rolled off her tongue like a whip lashing out to break my spirit. She would call me a bitch when she was angry. Those words became a self-fulfilling prophecy because I would live my life very coldly and disregard anyone else's feelings. The enemy lay in wait on every word she spoke. Over the length of my childhood the enemy gained an arsenal of weapons to use against me. Many times he would use these weapons in my adulthood in an attempt to destroy me.

As I reached adulthood I could not escape the enemies plan. The lies spoken over me had taken root and I began to believe them. I can remember saying to myself I can be a bitch if that's what she felt about me. Any peace and calm that I may have been able to enjoy as a child was destroyed early in my childhood. My heart was hardened and I showed no outer emotion. I lived nervously expecting to be hurt again. This expectancy became a normal state of life. I created circumstances that caused me pain by choosing unhealthy relationships. Even though I really did not want to be in those relationships I did nothing to avoid them. My expectations were so low for myself that I expected to experience abuse from people. The one thing that was not destroyed was my understanding that I was intelligent just like a horse. This belief had been my saving grace as a child and as an adult. I continued college courses and even earned a degree, but no level education would save from me from my choices. I had to discover that I had an inward strength that could not be destroyed. That inward strength was the same one that gave me strength to fight back as a child. It took me a long time before I would rediscover that strength. Once I did I began to live as though I believed it.

I had to turn my losses around in my favor. I had to turn what could have been weaknesses into step stools of victory. The more I walked in this inward strength the more freedom I found. I began to experience life in a new light. Life became more enjoyable. I was open to new life experiences. I stopped choosing relationships that were not moving me forward in my purpose. I lived now with the expectation of greatness. I knew I was created with great beauty. The change within me was reflected in the way I dressed, how I carried myself, and the social interactions I had with others. I could now live knowing and believing the beauty within is shining outwardly.

Do not be fooled, I still was not perfect. I am speaking now as I have seen the light at the end of the tunnel. Work continuously has to be done on my heart, but the stones have been broken away. Peace reigns and fear no longer controls my life. This will be the place where you will definitely be making some decisions to really stand firm on moving forward. You will have to accept that you are beautifully created. You have to realize that you have not been crushed at this point in your journey and you will make it. It takes you making a conscious choice to live above the pain of the past.

Turtle to Butterfly: A Journey Through My Self Discovery

1. What would you consider to be your greatest strengths?

2. In what ways are you beautiful?

3. In what ways can you create a peace within yourself? In your environment?

4. What can you do to start moving forward?

"He heals the wounds of the brokenhearted and binds up their wound."
Psalm 147:3-The Living Bible

Turtle to Butterfly: A Journey Through My Self Discovery

9 BUTTERFLY

RELEASED FROM HER COCOON SHE IS NOW FREE TO SOAR MANIFESTING THE BEAUTY CREATED IN TIME PAST.
GRETA MOON

The caterpillar spends its days in preparation for the next phase in its life which leads it to becoming a butterfly. Its beginning seemingly so plain and so insignificant yet birthing forth beauty. The butterfly begins to soar high expressing the glorious colors within its wings. As it flutters from flower to flower it helps to bring new life.

I often asked myself, "Why did it take me so long to get to this point in my life." At times I thought that I would not reach this point. I could not fly because they weight of my past was so great that it had to be shed in the process of metamorphosis. I shut off all emotion so I could not even hear God beckoning me into the cocoon. I can look back and see many wounds inflicted that were designed to thwart the promise of becoming this butterfly. There are many times that it seems I had to be reborn in a sense. I would die an emotional death and had to start the caterpillar process over again. The wounds of the past were so great that it seemed that the metamorphosis would never come. Even the process of changing was slow and arduous. Living in this caterpillar stage was not an easy task because I spent most of my life living below what I was created to become. Fear of letting go of that familiar life was so great that it kept me imprisoned within the caterpillar. I could not see myself finally being free to experience the metamorphosis. The journey has not been easy and I could not see beyond my present situations. I was a caterpillar and it seemed I was destined to stay that way. It is quite ironic that even though I did not see myself become that butterfly many others saw it long before its manifestation. They would speak words of a change in my life straight from the Creators lips and I would dismiss it every time. I spent many years moving slowly toward becoming a butterfly and then drawing back.

Even when the enemy was in full force I was learning to become a butterfly. God was going to use the time I vowed to be alone to gently draw me into the cocoon with His love. Slowly I began to allow process of transformation to begin. There was an unexpected part in this process that I did not realize had to occur. There had to be a death to the old life. The death of hurts, disappointments, lies spoken over me, and anger. I grieved for many weeks because I lived so many years within that caterpillar that she became my closest friend. As the death process begun I struggled initially to allow her to die. I was unsure of what my new life would look like, if I could live without the old Greta, and even if I truly was a butterfly. Once I began to shed the skin of the past something more glorious began. I begin to see the colors of my gifts and talents begin to appear. As the grieving process began to wane excitement started to build. I was ready to be free from the cocoon to soar in the earth.

The day came when it was time for me to break free from the cocoon. I could feel the skin of the chrysalis begin to split. I began to push outward stretching my wings allowing the sun to dry out anything that remained of the past. I sat upon the branch taking in this new life. Life looked more beautiful from this perspective. I crept forward in preparation of my first flight into my new life. Then I took off to soar higher and higher. All the colors in my wings expresses what God created for me to accomplish in the earth. I was overwhelmed with joy. For the first time I understood that I had a unique purpose to accomplish in the earth. I wake up every day in expectancy of God's love being more real and tangible in my life. Every day from that point forward my life has been so beautiful. I can love, live, and laugh without the chains of my past holding me back. There is an expectation to see what adventure every day holds. I look forward to seeing the impact that I have made and will make in the lives of others. Every gift and talent finally is shining with every ray of sun that shines upon my wings. It brings me great joy to use my gifts and talents to help others to see life is beautiful. Now that I know I am valuable I can speak value over other people. This freedom to soar manifesting beauty upon the earth is glorious. It so much freedom to live life and enjoy each day. I have begun to really understand why I am on this earth. I can walk confidently with my head held high because I know that I have worth.

You may be afraid to move forward allowing God to bring forth the beautiful butterfly you were meant to become. You were not meant to stay a caterpillar for the rest of your life. You have too much to contribute in this world. The world is waiting for you to become the butterfly to express your ideas, inventions, and knowledge. As long as you continue to live as a caterpillar you cannot make progress. Don't fool yourself into believing that you are living the fullness of your life because there is much more to experience. Many more people need to hear your story to help them become a beautiful butterfly. Surrender to the drawing into the cocoon so the process of transformation can begin. Let that dying process begin so that your life can burst from your chrysalis. You are unique and needed in the earth not to just exist, but to live. See yourself soaring above the chains of your past. Joy will overtake you. The sweetness of life will consume you and I can promise you that you will never look back to the days of being caterpillar.

One thing that I want to leave with you is to fill in the wings of this butterfly with the things that make you unique.

"Therefore, if anyone is in Christ, the new creature has come: The old is gone, the new is here!"
                2 Corinthians 5:17-New International Version

About the Author

Greta E. Moon is the mother of four children: Alexis, 28 Kaitlin, 25 Kendall 22, and Josiah 8 yrs. old. She currently lives in Chattanooga, TN. When she is not writing she enjoys spending time outdoors hiking and camping. She holds a degree in Biblical Studies from the International College of Bible Theology.

Greta has helped lead a teaching and worship conference for over 800 youth in Nakuru, Kenya. She has been to Acuna, Mexico to build a clinic and distribute food to the poor.

Greta has worked stateside on several mission projects building relationships with the homeless populations to provide clothing, outdoor gear, food, and other essentials in Missouri, Arkansas, and Tennessee.

She is currently establishing relationships with homeless women and children providing items necessary for them to transition from shelters to homes and building relationships of encouragement and hope.

She posts daily hope and inspiration on Facebook at Turtle to Butterfly, on Twitter at http://twitter.com/trtl2buttrfly.com, and on Google+ at Turtle to Butterfly.

www.ingramcontent.com/pod-product-compliance
Lightning Source LLC
Chambersburg PA
CBHW051713090426
42736CB00013B/2676